THE INS AND OUTS OF BECOMING A PHONE SEX OPERATOR

Elaine Shuel

Copyright 2011 Elaine Shuel

Notes:

I0393503

THE INS AND OUTS OF BECOMING A PHONE SEX OPERATOR

TABLE OF CONTENTS

INTRODUCTION

First off, let me start by saying that what you'll read about in this book, is about my experiences as a phone sex operator. I can't speak for all the phone sex operators out there. It doesn't mean it will be the same for you. I will discuss the types of calls I do and have done for the last 6 years. Whenever possible, I will give tips on what I've learned from doing my calls. Don't expect me to give out names of companies I've worked for. I don't name names. This book isn't to show you what companies to work for or to avoid. You have to determine that for yourself.

This is an insider look at what's involved in being a phone sex operator. PSOs are what we're called. Decide for yourself after reading this, is being a PSO something you really would enjoy doing? Is it something you'd be good at? I want it to get you thinking about what type of character you think would most fit your personality and voice. I consider phone sex the best part-time job since the money is great and if you love talking on the phone to men, it's a win-win situation. Full-time is another matter. To make real money, you need to be available often or you'll lose your customers. There are weeks you'll make huge amounts of money and other times, next to nothing. It's hard if that's your only source of income. I would advise keeping your other job if you have one, until you're sure you could afford to drop it. Try phone sex part-time and see what happens.

1. DIFFERENT TYPES OF PHONE SEX JOBS

I did phone sex working for an employer and others where I was considered a freelance contractor. One of my jobs involved doing virtual sex. The latter sometimes involved the phone but other times did not. I worked for a company that is the stereotype that sickened me and finally, I am self-employed working in association with a hosting company. The latter is by far the best choice if you like to be able to control your own characters. Let me explain each of those options.

A. WORKING FOR AN EMPLOYER

Like any other job, **be careful** who you work for. I was lucky that I was never cheated but my employer made "mistakes" on my paycheques regularly. When I would point them out, she would include the omission in the next cheque she sent. That's better than some. I have heard horror stories of companies owing quite a bit of money and closing down. The PSOs never got their pay.

Percentages vary of course. I received 50% of what a caller paid. Some companies pay more but most pay less. You must have a phone to do phone sex. No surprise there. Unless you are very lucky, you must pay for your own phone line. Your boss should set up a toll-free number for you and forward the calls to your number. Tips from clients were best. I received 90% and my employer received 10%. I am sure employers vary on those amounts but it gives you an idea of what is out there.

Trolling was something I had to do for myself. That means that I had to do the work to get my name out there, to find new clients. The company did some advertising but not that much. I went and chatted all over the place, discreetly of course. Sites often will ban you from a chat room if you advertise. The best way is to chat privately and give out your information to interested parties only.

When you work for an employer, you take on a phone sex character in most cases. I've heard of some companies that work differently. They use a dispatcher like you'll read about later. Taking on a character is very important. You really have to know what age you want that role to be and what characteristics she should have. Men often ask me if they could be a PSO and the answer is yes but usually they must be willing to suck cock for gay men and take it up the ass. The reality is that women calling phone sex lines are pretty rare. I have had some lesbians or bisexual women call but I could use my 10 fingers to list them all. Women usually talk to men for free when they want phone sex so why would they pay?

B.INDEPENDENT CONTRACTOR

VIRTUAL SEX

I did freelance work for one of those 3D virtual world sites where sex is done using avatars. The way it works at many phone sex companies is you don't work for them as an employee. After all, they would owe you vacation pay and have to add you to their payroll. Most have you work for them as a freelance contractor. That way they owe you absolutely nothing, except for the work you do for them. NO benefits at all.

I went to work for a company based in NYC and they didn't impress me. They are the ones that set me up in the virtual bordello and I was a virtual "working girl" there. Like real life working girls, I approached men to try to have sex with them for money.

Let me tell you something. Virtual sex is hard work, no pun intended. What makes it so tiring is that for virtual sex, you have to type and type and type. The guy agrees to do it and then both of you head to the bedroom in this 3D world. There is a bed and furniture and I have to admit that some of it seemed so real. I loved doing it with a black avatar. I kid you not. When his avatar licked my avatar's pussy, I got into the whole scenario. I'm like that on my calls too. I like to make it real in my mind.

Things were going really well there for a bit. I was one of the most popular girls working in the bordello because I did something that few others did. No, I don't mean sex acts that others wouldn't do. We were limited to the sexual activities that our virtual characters were able to do. What made me unique was that I typed out the words my avatar uttered, versus a script that I could have just clicked on. I wanted it to be as genuine as possible, typing what I was thinking, as I imagined doing the actions my avatar was engaged in. It added credibility to our sexcapade.

Virtual sex paid less than talking on the phone. It's suitable for you if you love to type for long periods of time, rapidly coming up with things or you don't mind being a robot using scripted words. Otherwise, virtual sex is something I would steer clear of. I've heard that recently where I worked, they stopped paying working girls with cash so if you want to try it, find out what and if they pay. After awhile, I had virtual sex with practically all the men that frequented the virtual whorehouse and things died down a bit. My boss got jealous because there was a guy she used to do it with and she got upset that he told her point blank that he preferred me. She ended up keeping my tips and she actually told me straight out that she did it since business slowed down. I quit that job since I don't like working for thieves. At least my past employer used to pay me what she owed me when I caught her "errors", that coincidentally were always in her favor.

The moral of my story is be careful who you work for, as an employee or as an independent contractor. There are honest people out there and ones that would cheat you without batting an eyelash.

PHONE SEX WITH NO TROLLING

I wanted to supplement my phone sex income because things got quiet at times. I thought I would try and see what it would be like to work for a company that wouldn't involve me trolling. Again, trolling is when you have to seek out new clients for yourself.

It's hard work and boring at times. Chatting with strangers and bringing up your work, trying to get them to do a call, isn't something that appeals to everyone. I love men but I don't like soliciting business.

I had heard that some women just lie on their backs and get calls. Sounded worth a try right? WRONG. I got a freelance job working for such an establishment. The pay was disgustingly low. It was less than 25 cents a minute. They charged clients more than any company I worked for and I got paid less.

It was very dull. There wasn't any soliciting clients, which was a plus. They do the advertising to get callers. In fact, we weren't allowed to generate business and there would have been no point. The caller could end up on the phone with any PSO. I lay down on my bed and waited for calls. I waited and waited and waited. You never knew when someone would call and I didn't want to miss a call by being at my computer. Later in the day, I did go to my desktop since I couldn't take lying around waiting. I answered the phone then went into my bed. I had no control about how many calls and it was the most tiresome position I ever had.

To make matters worse, we were told NOT to have sex with those that called in, for as long as possible. We were supposed to do anything but that. Talk about the weather, their families, anything to keep them on the line. Sound familiar, like the old stereotype about phone sex operators? That does work if you don't care about clients or like phone sex. The client stays on longer. The company is happy and eventually the customer gets off but not in the way they should if you know what I mean. They left dissatisfied and I felt terrible they didn't get what they paid for.

There is also no build up of clientele. You aren't the same character. In fact, you don't have a character. The dispatcher tells you what the caller is looking for. She is told that directly from the client when he calls in. You are then told what age or what criteria the client has and you become that persona. Let's say you have great rapport. He is crazy about you and you enjoyed talking to him. Wonderful, the odds that you will get to talk to him again are practically nil. It's only if he happens to call in at a time that you are on and the call is assigned to you. Otherwise, you'll never get to speak to him again.

To me, phone sex is about making money sure but it's also that I love talking to men. I've enjoyed the calls I've had with women too because I've had fantasies along those lines. That's not for everyone and it's a decision you must make for yourself. My goal is to earn a living but also to satisfy the men I talk to. I like giving pleasure and I'd like to think that after talking to me, they leave with a smile on their face. Finishing a call with a guy not getting to have any sexual fun when he wants it, I found to be very wrong and frankly disgusting. I quit after one day and I am not a quitter by nature.

WORKING FOR YOURSELF

I can't speak for everyone but when I did virtual sex and phone sex with no trolling, it wasn't as an employee. I did it as an independent contractor. Despite that, I still had bosses. I presently work for myself and I have no boss telling me what to do. With that comes some advantages and some disadvantages. To me, the advantages far outweigh the negatives.

Like any other job that you do on your own, I choose my own hours. While that was true when I had an employer, there were minimum hours a week expected, as was the case for the non-trolling position. No boss means you decide when you want to work. There are things that you have to do when you are on your own, that you usually don't have to do as an employee. One of those things involves finding a picture that will be what your character looks like. There are adult content providers and they sell nonexclusive rights to use the pictures of models they have in their portfolios. Typically, your rights extend to the internet only. You look at the poses of the women and the prices and how many pics and you decide what to buy. Generally the shoots include less than 100 photos. It shouldn't cost more than about $50 -$100 and for me, that was the entire investment to do it on my own. I bought 2 shoots so I'd have enough pictures of my character to display on my site and to send to clients. Different poses showing various body parts are best. Some men are into seeing a woman's behind. Other men want pussy pics. There are also guys with foot fetishes. The greater the variety, the more likely you'll have what they request.

Phone sex is harder to administrate than it used to be. Some credit card companies are cracking down on adult businesses and I've been affected at more than one job. Twice it happened to me that there was a temporary shutdown of a merchant account so we couldn't take calls. Thankfully it probably affected me a total of about 6 weeks in 6 years. If you work hand to mouth, meaning each week you use up all your money, you may have a problem if this happens to you. I suggest keeping a nest egg for rainy days.

Depending on what you want to do, you could either setup a toll-free number yourself and do all the admin for your calls or do what I did. Find an honest company to host your site, hopefully build a website for your character, and though you still make the ultimate decisions, they will do all the admin.

That doesn't mean you don't have to submit your calls. Every job requires that except those that you do the calls through a dispatch type of arrangement, depending on their setup. The other exception involves services that forward the calls to your phone, when guys see your online listing at their site. You must setup the account and put up a character's pic and do a profile page for each of your listings. You put yourself to available when you are ready to take calls. Men call you if they are interested. Make your profiles as enticing as possible so they'll want to call.

There are fees those companies deduct and at some of them, you earn about 70% if you sign up with them directly. You determine what to charge a client and there is no block of time. The client pays per minute. When I worked for my employer, callers paid for a block of time. Often that is 10 minutes or 15 minutes at one price and 30 minutes and/or an hour at another discounted price. $1.99 a minute used to be the basic charge when I started. I remember my boss warning me that if you charge less, you set up the notion that you aren't a good phone sex operator and you'll never be able to charge a decent price. I never charged less than $1.99 a minute. Google phone sex sites and I'm sure you'll get ideas of what to charge. Remember that if you charge too much or too little, you could lose out in the long run.

For me, I decided that I didn't want to do admin, other than sending out info about my calls and of course, my private note taking. I have to get authorization from the credit card company before a call begins and while I was able to do that for years over the phone, lately I've had to switch to getting the call approved over the internet. Find out upfront what way you would have to get your calls approved, at whatever organization you deal with, assuming the method affects you. Keep in mind, that things could change. They did for me. You have to adapt to changing circumstances in this line of work.

You may wonder why it matters what method is used, over the phone or over the internet. It did for me. When you take calls during the night, that depends on if you will, you will have to go to your computer and open it half asleep and get approval. I found it easier just using my phone on my nightstand and doing a 1-minute call to get authorization before the paid time.

When you work for yourself, depending on the arrangement you make with the hosting company, be prepared you might have to pay the line charges for any calls that come in. That is whether or not the caller decides to pay for a call. Not every call translates into a paid one. In fact, probably 9/10 calls will be calls to get information or just to hear your voice. When I talk about the line charges, I don't mean the $1.99 a caller would pay for the call. I mean the charges the phone company charges, like 5 cents a minute from Canada to USA, for example.

You might have to pay for the pictures yourself. You may even have to pay for the website. Find a good company like I did and hopefully they'll do the website free, providing you end up doing a sufficient amount of calls. He takes a cut, there's no getting away from that and it's only right. Bottom line is look at other phone sex websites and check out your competition. See what they are offering and be competitive, unless you feel fine with charging more or less. Ultimately, it's up to you. Anything under $20 for 10 minutes, in my opinion, isn't worthwhile. It might work for you but for most, they wouldn't take the call.

2. THINGS YOU NEED TO CONSIDER

WHAT AGE DO YOU WANT YOUR CHARACTER (S) TO BE?

Whether you work for yourself or for an employer, there are crucial decisions to make. Consider if you want to play a barely legal girl or someone in her 30s usually called a MILF. That acronym stands for mother I'd like to fuck. There are even GILFs, grandmother instead of mother. I have been amazed at how well some characters in their 60s and 70s do. Make sure your voice fits the age you choose. Think about this: you talk to a guy and you're pretending to be 18. Your voice and maturity makes it pretty obvious you are at least 35. You think he'll call you again. Forget it, he won't. Even though many clients are intelligent enough to know that you might not be what you advertise, they want to pretend it's true when you chat. Some men find out the truth and they are fine with it. Others get very upset when they realize they've been duped. Remember this is entertainment for the caller. They want to have a good time and they want to be satisfied. It is your job, your #1 priority to make them leave happy.

ACCENT OR NO ACCENT?

Accents are sexy, aren't they? Yes they could be. They could also sound phony if they aren't authentic and you aren't great at faking them. Nothing is more of a turn-off than pretending you're an Aussie and you're born and bred in Brooklyn, NY and it's evident when you talk. There are some that could get away with it. I had a co-worker who sounded like a Brit and she was a Canadian like me. She'd never been to the UK, let alone been born or lived there. She was a natural.

I have been told that my voice is distinctive. There is no way I would attempt to sound differently. I couldn't if I tried. You think you'd like to pretend you have an accent with callers? Test it on others first and see what happens. Best to find out that way then to establish yourself as something you can't live up to. Basically, I can't stress enough how your voice should fit your character. I've had guys tell me that I sounded like they expected from my pic. Now given I am three different characters, ranging in age from late 20s to my age early 50s, I take it as quite an achievement.

BODY TYPE

Make sure you're comfortable being the body weight that your character is. I am a BBW, meaning big beautiful woman. I wouldn't want my characters to be that. Perhaps it hits too close to home but if a guy would talk about big thighs or big anything, I would cringe. Having a niche could be quite good for phone sex. I know of one girl who did great being a supersized BBW.

BACKGROUND HISTORY AND PRESENT LIFE

My former employer and I disagreed on this topic but only to a degree. She told me to create a background for my character and her present living arrangements and not to use my actual one. I felt that the best thing would be to keep things as honest as I could. Therefore, against her better judgment, my first character was myself. Her name and pic wasn't me but everything else was. Whatever I told customers about my history was true. My education, experiences, everything was totally real. I think that came through during my calls. I had several clients fall in love with me and I think it is because they got to know me, not a fake person.

I ended up taking on two additional characters but not right away. It is best to start with one character. Take on another if/when you are ready to. You do need a separate number for each. I have two phones and an ident-a-call number on one; three phone numbers that could be called on in total. In fact, I have all three personas to this day. The other two, I did have to make up backgrounds for. They are not my age and it would not have been possible they lived my life.

Not one person has fallen in love with either of those two characters, even though both were popular when I did them actively. Lately, I've been concentrating more on my writing so my phonesex has taken a backseat somewhat. I think it boils down to, clients want to get a real sense of the person they are talking to. I don't think reality bites. I think reality sells. My former employer held some contests and I won all of them. She stopped having contests. Is it because I'm the best phone sex operator of them all? No. It's because I never faked things. I gave them myself during the time we talked. The other girls weren't being themselves.

WHAT TYPE OF CALLS COULD YOU HANDLE?

Generally there is a connection between the type of character you will assume and the type of calls you will get. My MILF role gets many incest calls, guys who want to pretend they are doing it with their moms. Can't handle that? Don't choose to be a MILF. Barely legal girls won't get many older woman/younger man type calls. Their calls will have many of the reverse, young girls/older men.

There are calls that you never knew about and some will be so distasteful to you, you'll refuse to do them. There's nothing wrong with that. That would be a problem if you refuse to do many calls. That would mean you either aren't suited to be a phone sex operator or you picked the wrong age or look for your woman.

Could you do BDSM calls? Those who roleplay as dominant women, taking calls from men who want to be submissive, often do well. The more extreme the methods they use, example CBT that stands for cock and ball torture, the better they do. I am not personally into major pain and punishment so though I've done some mild BDSM calls, it's not really my forte. I have to admit that I have changed somewhat though in recent times and probably could take on harsher forms of BDSM. Just think about the fact you aren't hurting anyone and the guy is getting off on it.

Hypnosis is another area that could be quite lucrative. It's not for me but it could be for you. I have a hard time believing that one's voice could control someone so when I do such a call, I'm not into it. I could tell the guy I attempted it with, didn't have a great time. I like my clients to feel they got their money's worth or I'm unhappy. Based on that, I have refused callers who tell me upfront they want to do a hypnosis call.

Feminization calls could be fun. These men love to dress up as women and I do get excited for them. You could tell how much they enjoy it and I am pleased to be part of liberating them, even if for a short time. Some like us to go over their outfits and I've had conversations talking about what shoes they should wear. Think about if those types of calls would appeal to you. You could always try one call like that and see.

Humiliation calls are rough at first. I had a caller tell me about his cock being smaller than the baby of a woman he met. He told me he couldn't get a date his entire life because of it and he wanted me to insult him. For me this was very difficult. I cried throughout the call. I spoke to my then boss and she explained that they get pleasure out of being put down so I should look at it that I am not hurting them. It is making them feel better. I started thinking of it that way and it helped. I do remember one time I had a guy over; this was before I met my boyfriend. He was at my house and he was about to lick my pussy. The phone rang and he told me to get it. I answered the phone and did a call while my slit was being eaten out. It turned out to be a humiliation call. Here I was insulting the guy and moaning. It was weird. The guy and I laughed after that call.

Interracial scenarios turn me on and so do gangbangs. Think about if you feel comfortable doing those calls. You must be open-minded and put yourself in the moment, otherwise this job isn't for you.

Sex with underage children isn't for everyone. I obviously don't mean in real life, where it's illegal and not acceptable, period. I mean in phone sex. Some women will do such calls and others can't stomach it. You have to decide what your boundaries are.

Of course, there are many other types of calls you could get. It would be impossible to list all of them. You will need to think quickly. Those who can't come up with things to respond to unusual or unexpected situations, won't last.

QUALITIES NEEDED AND OTHER THINGS TO CONSIDER

You need to be a good listener. Ask the caller what fantasies they have and what turns them on. Some want a scenario acted out. Others like to get right down to business. The aim is to turn them on not you. If you are turned on too, it's a bonus. It doesn't matter if you like to talk first or the scenario he wants doesn't appeal to you. It's their money and they are the ones you need to put first.

You must have a voice that men want to listen to. I remember being told that at my company a girl did terrible. Seems she had a voice that was unappealing for phone sex. Honestly, I don't care for my voice but men told me they love it and my employer told me it was well suited to doing phone sex. That's ultimately what matters. Have other men judge your voice to see if it's sexy.

Good setup in your house. You need a place to do phone sex. I heard the old stereotypes, women working in cubicles in an office all moaning. That isn't the way it is. It might have been like that in the past but not since I began. My room is where I conduct my phone sex calls. You need a place where you won't be interrupted. You don't want to be in the middle of a call and your young son or daughter comes in and talks to you. I lie on my bed, which is next to my phone. For me, my tools of the trade are my sex toys. Don't expect all calls to make you wet and horny. It isn't the case. Some will and some won't. That's when my toys come into play. Your fingers could do the same.

16

I use my dildos or silver bullets, fucking machine or rabbits or my favorite magic wand, whatever I'm in the mood for, during calls. When I'm having a good time, it enhances the experience for me. This translates into more pleasure for my phone lover. The more I moan, the more excited he gets. There are guys that don't care about getting you off. I have found that most do care. They really want to give you a good time too.

You need to be vocal. Just like few like to watch porn with a practically lifeless quiet woman, phone sex needs women who are able to express themselves uninhibitedly. You may be feeling wonderful and ready to cum but if you don't scream out, how does he know that? He won't like the call, believe me. Let me tell you a tip. Use the guy's name whenever possible. "Ohhhhhhhhhh Mike, I love your hard cock" will get you much farther than "Hey baby, your cock feels great." It gives a personal touch.

You need to like to talk to men. I don't mean to just have sex with them. There are guys that are lonely and just want to talk to a caring woman. Many believe that guys who call phone sex lines are all desperate and pathetic. That is so far from the truth, it's amazing. There are some that would fit the bill but they are in the minority. What phone sex offers is a safe form of excitement for those who aren't getting enough in their relationships or for those who always need more. They don't want to cheat on their significant others but they need the extra interaction of a woman that won't complicate their lives. Some are between relationships. They want someone to connect with and don't feel comfortable having sex with hookers or one-night stands. There are men away on business trips and you know what they say, "when the cat is away, the mice will play." Here the men are away and they like to play.

You need to be available. When I started, I worked 24/7 when I was home, seriously. I kept the phone on all night and took calls at all hours. It wasn't the healthiest thing to do and I wouldn't recommend that. It was good for my income but I think overall, not a wise thing to do for one's well-being. That said, don't devote 1 hour a week and expect to be earning enough to live on. You get out of it what you give. Like all businesses, it takes time to build up clientele. Some become regulars but that doesn't mean they'll call you daily. More likely some will call you every few days or every week or every month. There are those that will call even less often. You will lose your regulars if you aren't around much. They'll try to reach you but eventually, they'll move on to a PSO who is more readily available.

Don't be jealous. This is easier said then done. We're all human and when a guy decides to go to another woman, it hurts in some cases. When I worked at my former company, sometimes I did know when a guy switched to another woman at the same company. Often they'd flock to the new woman who just started there. They liked fresh meat. Of course, I got some guys that didn't want to continue with my co-workers and switched to me. It all balances out. You can't take it personally. Some stick to you for a long time and then leave. Having them fall in love with you is the kiss of death. Expect to lose that client. He'll want to meet you and if you refuse over and over again, chances are he will get fed up and leave.

My boss told me and I will pass the same warning on to you. The cardinal rule is not to meet any clients in person. Despite the warning, some women have met up with their callers, including me. A handful of men became personal friends, getting to know the real me. I met only one in person since the others don't live in my province. It was a long process and under various circumstances I gave them my personal phone number. I didn't do phone sex with them unless they paid. That's important or some guys will be your "friend" in order to get phone sex calls for free. I wouldn't advise meeting in person with any clients, unless you know what you are doing. I have great instincts and they haven't steered me wrong. It is a risk and you do not want to be wrong and have a stalker in your life. Be careful!

Make sure your significant other is fine with you doing phone sex for money. I have talked to women who really wanted to do phone sex and then the closer they came to beginning the job, their real life partners couldn't handle it. They didn't end up doing it. Don't waste your time or anyone else's time until you're sure it's

18

ok with your partner or if it isn't, you're fine with going against their wishes.

You need a vivid imagination. When a guy pays for a 10 or 15-minute call, he doesn't want you to spend most of it coming up with a scenario. Think about the guy and what his likes and dislikes are, if he's a regular. Take notes on ALL new callers on everything about him that you recall. Use that as a reference until you get to know him better and remember those things. There are guys that don't want to do scenarios or those that will tell you exactly what they want you to act out. Others will challenge you to come up with a great roleplaying event. It will be your job to do that.

Using new words to describe the same scene is hard to do but necessary. Would you like me to use pussy every moment? Men don't want pussy used 100 times in one call. You will get guys that will tell you they love the word "cunt". Does that word bother you? Are you able to say cock and prick, dick and …? You get my drift. Dirty talk is what it's about and if that makes you uncomfortable, this isn't for you. Let's say you speak to a client and he says he hates the word cock. He likes the word prick used. Take note of that and avoid using cock and stick in some pricks in your conversation.

You have to be comfortable talking dirty. What I just wrote in the prior paragraph is what I mean. You have to talk nasty and the nastier the better with some men. Others won't like getting down and dirty. You'll get to know the callers and what they want. It's not the same for everyone. They all have their own tastes. Different strokes for different folks, as they say.

3. STILL WANT TO BECOME A PHONE SEX OPERATOR?

I hope you now have a clearer understanding of what's involved in doing phone sex. There are no lessons on how to do the actual phone sex. My first boss told me that. She was correct. We all do it differently and there is no right way and no wrong way. What I try most to do is to keep it real. Use toys or fantasize or anything you need to turn yourself on, especially if your call isn't doing that. Make your moans come from your body, not fabricated. When you feel aroused and you let out your screams of ecstasy, your client will think it's from him even if it isn't. He'll get pleasure and so will you.

Decide if you want to work for someone or for yourself. The pay should be higher when you do it on your own but there are usually more expenses. Overall you should still come out ahead and have greater control over your own character. After all, you bought the pictures of the model you preferred and chose her name. You gave life to her, not in the way of giving birth of course but deciding on who she is and what she likes and who her family is and everything else involving her.

Most importantly, think about if this job is really for you. You will lose your clients if you aren't around when they call. Sure you could miss a call or two but if he calls and you're almost never there, he won't wait for you. Develop thick skin. Be prepared that some men will tell you how beautiful you are and they mean your character. I had a bit of an identity crisis at first but got over it. It's the nature of the job.

Be prepared to do some tasks like authorizing the call and depending on the company, sending them info to get paid for it. At some organizations, they go together, authorization automatically

20

sends them the info. Keep great notes on your clients. It's great when they speak to you and you remember who they are and things about them. We all like to feel special and it makes them feel like they were worth remembering.

Someone wrote a fictional story about a phone sex operator and she said something about not telling clients your deepest and darkest fantasies. I couldn't disagree more. What is wrong with sharing your innermost thoughts with those you develop a rapport with? I share a bit of myself with my closest clients and they do the same with me. They pay me for the call but other than that, I love the intimacy of what we share.

I recall that a co-worker of mine said she doesn't enjoy the calls anymore. She strictly did it to earn money. I don't consider that fair to the client but that said, as long as he's getting what he wants and so is she, it works. For me, I would get out completely if I didn't like it anymore. Trolling turns me off I must admit but the actual calls I wouldn't want to give up. Basically, being a phone sex operator is a great job but it takes work.

THE END

ABOUT THE AUTHOR:

Elaine Shuel has had a varied career. University educated, she has held several professional positions. Elaine has enjoyed using creativity to accomplish her goals. Writing erotic stories has been especially gratifying and challenging. She is the proud recipient of a 2010 Author Award at A1adultebooks. Elaine will continue surprising her readers with unexpected twists whenever possible.

Her work as a phone sex operator and erotic stories author, gives her the opportunity to stimulate both her readers and callers. Giving pleasure is her top priority and one she relishes doing.

Elaine feels that she has many facets to her personality that she likes to explore. While erotica gives her a chance to express her sexual side, she does enjoy writing about other topics that she has interest in. She has already written a fictional story for young adults called Mindy's Favorite Room. Ask Elaine is yet another book that is a departure from erotica. It is one she hopes will make a difference in someone's life, when making certain decisions. What means the most personally to Elaine, is her newest book Skippy, a fictional children's story written with the love she feels for her dog who died in 1988. He is forever in her heart.

ELAINE SHUEL ONLINE:

E-mail: shuel_2000@yahoo.ca

Yahoo Messenger: shuel_2000

MSN Messenger: shuel2002@hotmail.com

Website http://elaineshuel.com

SOME OTHER ELAINE SHUEL BOOKS:

- **Simon Says**
- **Taught A Lesson**
- **Brittany's Master**
- **BDSM Tetralogy**
- **My Wife's A Gangbang Addict**
- **My Neighbour, The Nympho**
- **Taken For A Ride**
- **Caught In The Act**
- **Erotica Author Bares All**
- **How I Became A Phone Sex Operator – My True Story**
- **The Surprise**
- **Women Who Love Black Meat**

www.ingramcontent.com/pod-product-compliance
Lightning Source LLC
Chambersburg PA
CBHW071526180526
45171CB00002B/397